P9-DDS-800

D0015286

Sidewalk GAMES

Around the World

By Arlene Erlbach

Illustrated by Sharon Lane Holm

The Millbrook Press   Brookfield, Connecticut

Dedicated to Lettie Lee at the Ann Elmo Agency,
who really loved this project   A.E.

To Gregory   S.L.H.

Library of Congress Cataloging-in-Publication Data
Erlbach, Arlene.
Sidewalk games around the world / by Arlene Erlbach.
p. cm.
Includes bibliographical references.
Summary: Describes various games played by children
in countries around the world, describing the places
where the games are played and the directions and
equipment needed for each game.
ISBN 0-7613-0008-2
1. Games–Juvenile literature. [1. Games.] I. Title.
GV1203.E68 1997
796.1'4–dc20 96–8715 CIP AC

Published by The Millbrook Press, Inc.
2 Old New Milford Road
Brookfield, Connecticut 06804

Copyright © 1997 by Arlene Erlbach
Art copyright © 1997 by Sharon Lane Holm
All rights reserved
Printed in the United States of America
5 4 3 2 1

Contents

Acknowledgments

The author would like to thank the following people and organizations whose input helped make this book possible.

The Australian Tourism Commission
The Embassy of Bolivia
Consulate General of Britain
Canadian Consulate General
Embassy of Ethiopia
Consulate General of Haiti
Hong Kong Trade
Development Counsel
India Consulate General
Consulate General of Indonesia
The Iran Jewish Congregation of Skokie
Ahmad Zaki, Deputy Director, Malaysia
Tourism Promotion Board
Embassy of Mali
Mexican Trade Commission
Consulate General of the Netherlands
Embassy of Norway
Embassy of Pakistan
Scandinavian Museum
Esther Fillmore and the South African
Consulate General
Consulate General of Spain

Consulate of Thailand
Dr. Neil Aaronson and his friends
from Holland, Ysette Witteveen
and Brandon Graff
Karen Arnold
Farshad Davatgar
The Baci Family
John Edwards, who inadvertently gave
us a Mancala game for a grab bag at
a Christmas party
Herb Erlbach
Charlotte Herman
Debbie Herman
Niketa Parekh
Stina Peterson
Elyse Rasky-O'Connor and her cousins
from Argentina and Chile
Professor John S. Rohsenow, Department
of Linguistics, University of Illinois,
Chicago Circle Campus
Helene Wahleman, the Peterson's guest from
Sweden

Introduction

Every day, all over the world, children play games on sidewalks or outside their homes. They jump ropes, roll marbles, draw games on sand or cement, or chase each other, playing tag.

Some kids play in large groups. They form teams and try to win. Other children play with one or a few friends. Children from all parts of the globe play their games very much the way you play yours.

In this book, you'll learn how to play games that children play in other countries. Some games will be similar to games you already know. They may be the same games you play but with different rules. Other games will be new to you.

You'll discover unique ways to use sidewalk game gear like marbles, balls, jump ropes, and chalk. You'll learn how to make some game gear, too. You'll impress your friends by teaching them games they've never heard about.

Some of the games may be versions played in one part of a country or even in a certain neighborhood. So rules and methods of playing can be adapted to suit you and your friends.

While you're playing a game from *Sidewalk Games Around the World,* think about this: Other children, far across the globe, might be playing the same game you are playing.

Albania

Albania is one of the smallest countries in Europe. In Albania, many children live in small towns of 1,000 people or less that have narrow, winding streets. On one of the winding streets in each town is an outdoor

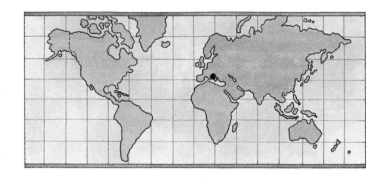

bazaar called a *treg*, where people buy food, spices, and cloth from street vendors.

Many of Albania's streets are unpaved, yet children still enjoy playing *varra* (pronounced *VAH-ruh*), a form of hopscotch. You can play *varra*, too. It's fun, because players can make up certain rules and jumps as they go along.

Varra

Number of players: 4 to 10

What you'll need: chalk

How to play:

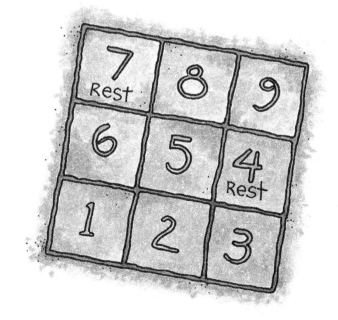

1. First draw the *varra* pattern. Each square should measure between 12 and 18 inches (30 and 45 centimeters) on each side. Number the squares.

2. Choose which two squares will be safe resting squares. These are places where you can put both feet down. You can decide on the resting squares with the other players.

3. To begin play, the first player attempts to hop on one foot from square 1 to square 9, stopping only on the safe squares, and without stepping on any lines.

4. If the first player makes it to square 9, he or she goes again—until he or she misses. But the game gets harder. Now other players can ask the player to hop backward, blindfolded, or with hands behind his or her back.

Many children count aloud as they hop from square to square. You can count aloud in English or, if you'd like to count in Albanian, here's how to do it:

Number	Albanian Word	How to Say It
1	një	nyu
2	dy	dee
3	tre	treh
4	katër	kah-TER
5	pesë	pes
6	gjashtë	josh
7	shtatë	stot
8	tetë	tet
9	nëntë	nunt

Argentina

Argentina is the second-largest country in South America. It occupies the southern tip of South America, so it's in the Southern Hemisphere. In Argentina, children have their summer vacation from the second week in December to the first week in March.

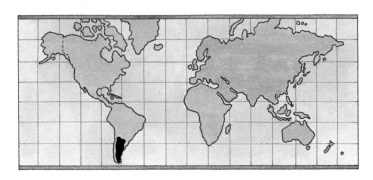

South American children enjoy games of skill, especially jump rope. One jump-rope game children play is *el reloj* (pronounced *el REL-lo*), which means "the clock." *El reloj* works best with lots of players.

El Reloj

Number of players: **4 to 10**

What you'll need: **a long jump rope**

How to play:

1. Two players hold the ends of a long jump rope and swing it.

2. Other players stand in line.

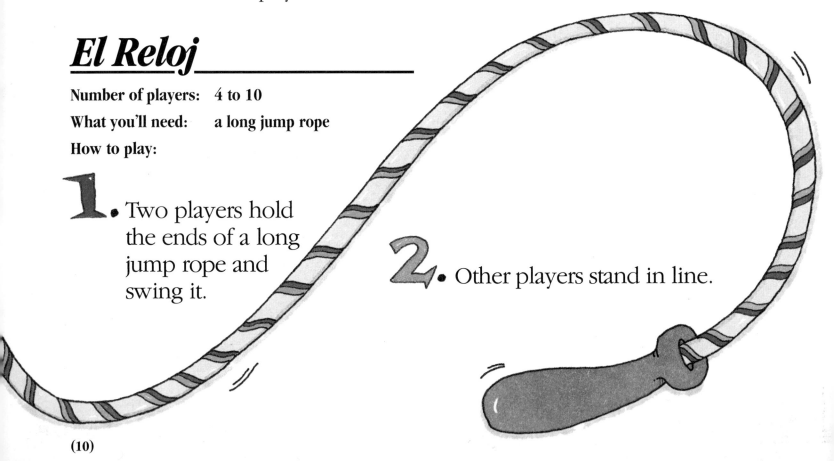

3. The first person **jumps** over the rope once, and says "one o'clock."

4. The second player **jumps** the rope twice and says "two o'clock."

5. The game continues until a player reaches twelve o'clock, and jumps the rope twelve times without missing.

You and your friends can shout the hours in English or in Spanish, which is the language spoken in Argentina.

English	Spanish	How to Say It
one o'clock	es la uno	ehs la OO-no
two o'clock	son las dos	sone lahs doce
three o'clock	son las tres	sone lahs trace
four o'clock	son las cuatro	sone lahs KWA-tro
five o'clock	son las cinco	sone lahs SING-ko
six o'clock	son las seis	sone lahs sace
seven o'clock	son las siete	sone lahs see-EH-tay
eight o'clock	son las ocho	sone lahs O-cho
nine o'clock	son las nueve	sone lahs noo-EH-vay
ten o'clock	son las diez	sone lahs DEE-es
eleven o'clock	son las once	sone lahs OHN-say
twelve o'clock	son las doce	sone lahs DOE-say

Australia

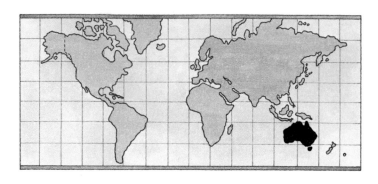

Australia is the only continent in the world that's occupied by just one nation. So it's often called the island continent. About a quarter of the world's wool comes from Australia.

Australia is located south of the equator. Its climate is warm and sunny. So children have lots of time to play outdoors. One game you'll see children playing is four square, which is similar to handball.

Four Square

Number of players: **4 and up**

What you'll need: **chalk**

                         a tennis ball

                         a yardstick

How to play with 4 players:

1. On Australian playgrounds, you may find four squares already painted onto cement, but you will have to draw your own.

2. On the pavement, use chalk to draw a big square that measures about 2 to 3 yards (1.75 to 2.75 meters) on each side. Divide the big square into four equal squares.

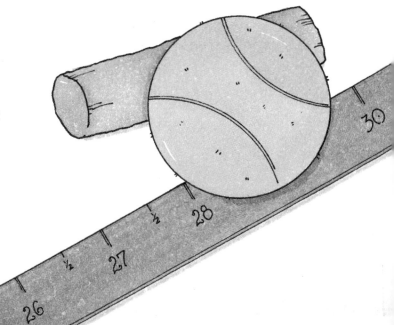

3. Mark the squares, King, Queen, Jack, Dunce as shown in the picture. The squares are ranked in that order. Each player stands inside one of the four squares.

4. The King bounces a ball from inside his square to either the Jack, Queen, or Dunce. The King must bounce the ball hard enough to reach its destination in one bounce.

5. The player who catches the bounced ball bounces it on to another player.

6. If the player who is bouncing the ball doesn't bounce it hard enough to get it into a square, that player is out. If the player to whom the ball is bounced misses it, that player becomes the Dunce.

7. Each of the other players who are not King move up a rank. So the Dunce becomes the Jack. The Jack becomes the Queen.

8. The object of the game is to keep moving up in rank to become the King. So players must try to get the King out.

There are no points to the game and no ending time. Players just keep bouncing the ball and try to get the King out or become King themselves.

Directions for more than 4 players:
Instead of becoming the Dunce, the player who makes an out is out of the game. The remaining 3 players move up in rank, leaving an empty Dunce square, and a new player enters as Dunce. Players continue play. Each time there's an out, the player who made an out is out of the game. Players move up in rank, and a new Dunce enters.

Bolivia

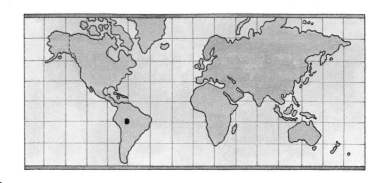

Bolivia is located in South America, and is bordered by Peru, Chile, Brazil, Argentina, and Paraguay. Bolivia has two main cities, La Paz and Sucre. Sucre is the official capital, where the supreme court is located. La Paz is where the seat of government is located.

Many Bolivian children are Indian. Their culture goes back thousands of years. These children speak two languages: their own Indian language and Spanish.

A popular Bolivian game is *tirar frijoles* (pronounced *TEE-rahr FREE-ho-les*), which means "throw the beans." Bolivian children play the game with dried beans. But if no beans are available, you may use marbles instead. There are many ways to play *tirar frijoles*. Here's one way to play it.

Tirar Frijoles

Number of players: 2

What you'll need: chalk

a bag of dried beans (or marbles) divided equally between the players

How to play:

1. Draw a line on the ground with chalk.

2. Each player stands about 5 feet (1.5 meters) from the line and attempts to flick a bean toward the line. The player whose bean lands closest to the line becomes the standing player. The other player becomes the kneeling player, who will be the first player to throw the beans.

3. The standing player stands by the line toes apart with a bean in his or her hand.

4. The kneeling player kneels about 5 feet (1.5 meters) from the line and attempts to flick a bean between the standing player's feet.

5. The kneeling player gets three attempts to land a bean.

6. If the kneeling player does not land a bean, the standing player keeps the unlanded beans, and takes a turn at being the kneeling player.

7. If the kneeling player lands a bean, the standing player drops the bean he or she is holding.

8. The kneeling player tries to hit the opponent's bean. If it's hit, the bean belongs to the kneeling player. If not, the standing player keeps the bean as well as the bean used for the hit.

The game ends when one player owns all the beans or marbles.

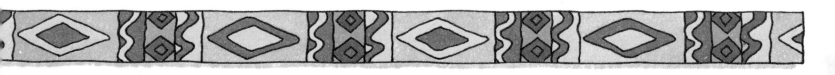

Canada

Canada is located north of the United States. It's the second-largest country in the world. Most Canadians speak English, but about one third of them consider French their native language.

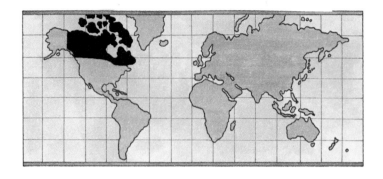

One of Canada's most popular sports is ice hockey. Many Canadian children play a version without ice, called ball hockey, on their sidewalks, playgrounds, or in their yards.

Ball Hockey

Number of players:	**4 to 12, divided into teams (or 2 players can play against each other)**
What you'll need:	**chalk**
	a tennis ball
	hockey sticks for each player (some Canadian children use brooms instead of sticks and call the game broom hockey)

How to play:

1. Decide where each team's goal should be. Mark a line there with chalk. The object of the game is to hit the ball behind the opposing team's goal.

2. Set the ball into the center of the playing area. Players attempt to hit the ball with their hockey stick or broom toward the opposing team's goal.

3. Opposing team players attempt to keep the ball away from their goal, or hit it toward the other team's goal.

4. A ball hit behind the opposing team's goal wins a point for the hitter's team.

The game ends when players decide to stop playing.

Here's how to add your points in French, the official language of the Canadian province of Quebec.

Number	French	How to Say It
1	un	uh
2	deux	duh
3	trois	trwa
4	quatre	KAT-re
5	cinq	sank
6	six	seece
7	sept	set
8	huit	weet
9	neuf	nuhf
10	dix	deece

Chile

Chile is a long narrow country located in western South America. It's so narrow that it measures only about 100 miles (160 kilometers) across in some places. So a person could drive across the country in about two hours. But it would take days to drive from north to south. Chile is about 2,000 miles (3,200 kilometers) long.

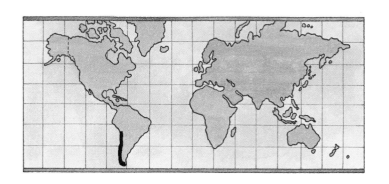

Chilean children love to play games outdoors. One game, played on the front steps of homes, is called *cielo, luna, mar* (pronounced *see-EL-lo LU-na mar*). The words mean "sky, moon, sea." The game is similar to Simon Says, except that it's played on steps with only two players.

Cielo, Luna, Mar

Number of players: 2

How to play:

1. Decide which steps will be the Sky, Moon, and Sea. You can label them with chalk if you want, or draw pictures on them.

2. Choose one player to be the caller. The other is the jumper.

3. The jumper stands at the bottom of the steps. The caller shouts "sea," "sky," or "moon."

4. The jumper jumps one step at a time onto the step called by the caller.

5. The caller keeps calling until the jumper misses.

6. Then the jumper becomes the caller.

Sea!

China

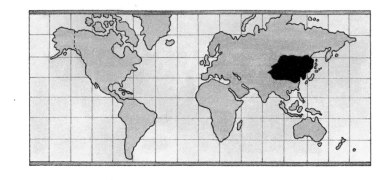

More than one billion people call China home. About one fifth of the world's population lives in China. It's the third-largest country on Earth.

In China, you probably would not have brothers or sisters. Most Chinese children are only children. The Chinese government encourages families to have just one child. So children are considered very special people.

Chinese children love to play games after school and on weekends. One favorite is *t'yow fang zi* (pronounced *tyow fahng zih*), a Chinese form of hopscotch. The words in Chinese mean "hopping house."

T'Yow Fang Zi

Number of players: at least 2

What you'll need: white and colored chalk

How to play:

1. Draw a large rectangle on the sidewalk or in your yard.

2. Divide the big rectangle into eight smaller rectangles. You'll have one big rectangle with eight smaller rectangles in it.

3. Number the smaller rectangles from 1 to 7. The space in the upper left hand corner is Public House. Players will need this space later to rest from hopping. Public House is like a free space.

4. Drop a stone into space 1. Hop in and pick up the stone.

5. If you complete the hop without touching a line, drop the stone into space 2. Hop in again.

6. A player keeps going until he or she hops into and picks up his or her stone in spaces 1 through 7, without stepping on a line.

7. A player who has gone through all seven spaces can mark off half of any space in colored chalk. This space is that player's Private House. When he or she plays again, that space can be used for resting, in addition to Public House.

8. The person who marks the most Private Houses wins. The game can end at a designated time, or when all the spaces become Private Houses.

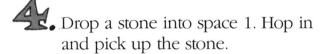

You can number your spaces from 1 to 7 or use Chinese numbers. Here's how they're written and how to pronounce them.

Number	Chinese	How to Say It
1	一	yee
2	二	uhr
3	三	sahn
4	四	suh
5	五	woo
6	六	lyo
7	七	chee

Ethiopia

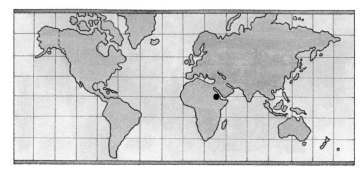

Ethiopia is located in eastern Africa, right on a bulge of land called the horn of Africa. Much of Ethiopia contains mountains. Addis Ababa, the capital, is more than a mile (1.6 kilometers) above sea level.

In Ethiopia a year has thirteen months. Ethiopian months are exactly thirty days long, so the extra days each year are used in a short month called *Pagame*. Every month, Ethiopians celebrate some type of festival.

Throughout the year, Ethiopian children and adults play a game called *gabata* (pronounced *geh-beh-TAH*). *Gabata* is a type of *mancala* game. *Mancala* games have been common in Africa for more than 3,000 years. People all over Africa play many forms of *mancala*, with slightly different rules. Here's how to play *gabata*, the *mancala* game common to Ethiopia.

Gabata

Number of players: 2

What you'll need:

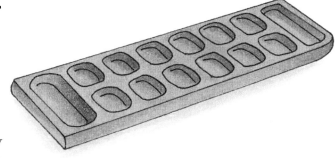

Ethiopian children play *mancala* games with a carved board that has six compartments on each side, and one larger compartment on each end. The object of the game is for each player to capture as many beads or pebbles as possible. Then players put them into the end compartments, which are called *mancalas*. You can purchase a *mancala* set—or you can play using an empty egg carton and 48 pebbles or stones. If you're using an egg carton, the *mancala* will be a space beside the egg carton.

How to play:

1. Each player puts four stones into each of the six compartments on his or her side of the board. Stones later captured will go into the *mancala* to the right of each player. If playing with an egg carton, the stones will be placed in a space to the right of the egg carton.

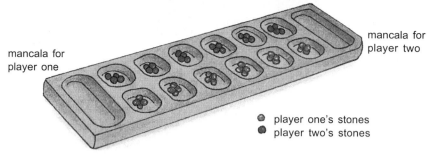

mancala for player one

mancala for player two

• player one's stones
• player two's stones

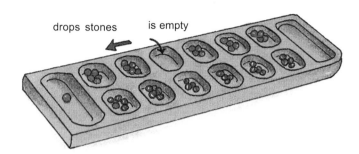

drops stones   is empty

2. The first player scoops up all four stones from one of the compartments on his or her side of the board. Then the player drops them, one by one, into compartments to his or her left or right. A player can go in only one direction on each turn.

3. Stones can be dropped into the player's own compartments, the opponent's compartments, or the player's own *mancala*. If a player reaches the opponent's *mancala*, he or she skips it. and continues to play, dropping the stones into the next compartments. A player's turn ends when he or she drops the last stone in his or her hand into a compartment.

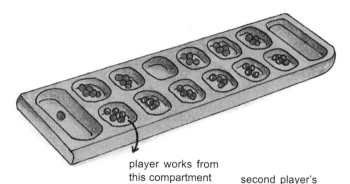

player works from this compartment

second player's possible play

4. If a player drops the last stone from his or her hand into a *mancala*, the player gets another turn.

5. When a player drops the last stone from a handful in an empty compartment on his or her side of the board, that stone goes into his or her *mancala*. Plus the player captures all the stones in the opponent's compartment directly across from where the last stone was dropped.

6. As the game progresses, some compartments will contain more than four stones. Some will contain fewer. Other compartments will become empty. Each player's *mancala* will fill with stones. So, as the game goes on, a player may pick up more or less than four stones, depending on which compartment the player chooses to play from. The game ends when one player's side of the board is emptied. The player with the most stones in his or her *mancala* wins.

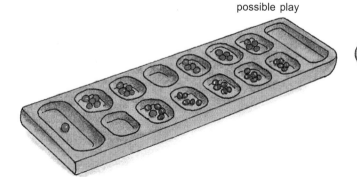

France

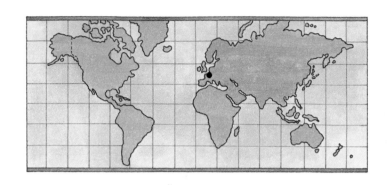

If you lived in France, your school day would be long. French schoolchildren usually go to school from 8:30 in the morning until 4:30 or 5:00 in the afternoon. But your lunch period would be two hours! On Saturday morning you might attend school, but on Wednesday you might only go until noon—or not at all.

At recess and after school, many French children play *les billes* (pronounced *lay beey*), the French word for marbles. Children play *les billes* many ways in France. Here's one way to play it.

Les Billes

Number of players: **2 to 6**

What you'll need: **chalk**

                      large and small marbles

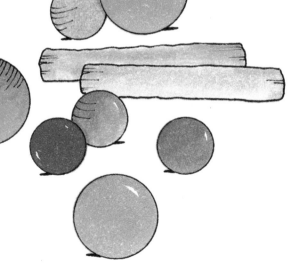
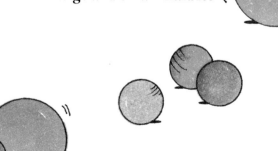

How to play:

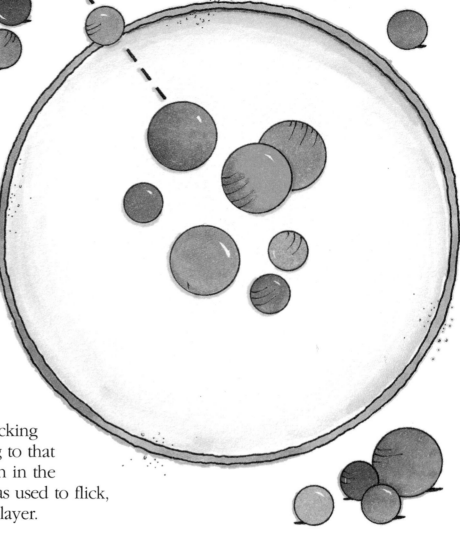

1. Draw a circle 10 to 12 feet (about 3 meters) in diameter.

2. Each player decides to place either one or two large marbles inside the circle.

3. The first player attempts to hit the marbles by flicking them with a smaller marble. The object is to hit one or both marbles outside of the circle in just one hard flick.

4. If any of the hit marbles roll outside the circle, the person flicking collects them. They then belong to that player. Whatever marbles remain in the circle, including the one that was used to flick, remain as a target for the next player.

5. The next player attempts to flick the marbles remaining in the circle out of the circle.

The game has no specific ending time. When no marbles remain in the circle, players put one or two marbles in the circle again.

The player who collects the most marbles wins.

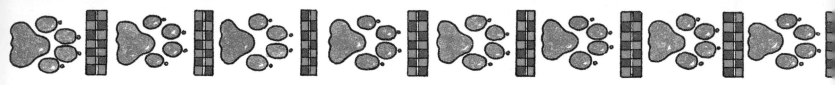

Great Britain

Great Britain includes England, Scotland, and Wales. Great Britain's population includes people from many countries and cultures.

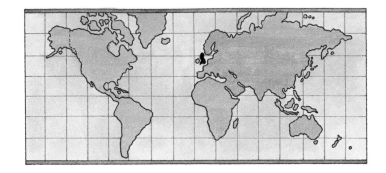

British people love animals. More than half of British families own pets, and their favorites are cats and dogs. One tag game that children play is named after a popular dog breed. It's called British Bulldog.

British Bulldog

Number of players: 4 to 10

How to play:

1. All players line up, facing one player who is It.

2. Players begin to run.

3. It attempts to tag these players.

4. Once players are tagged, they attempt to tag non-tagged players.

5. The last one to be tagged is the winner, or British Bulldog – and the game begins again.

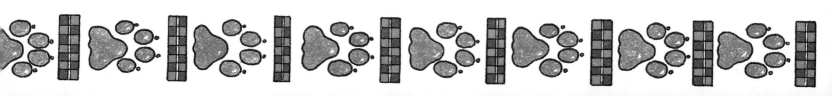

Haiti

Haiti is the second-largest island in the Caribbean. Its climate is hot and dry all year, so Haitian children have lots of good weather for playing outside. They play on their porches or in front of their homes.

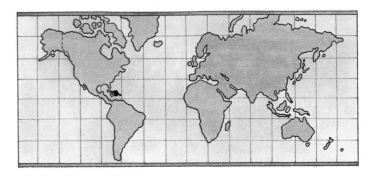

One very common game that Haitian children play is *osselets* (pronounced *OO-slay*). It's similar to jacks, but *osselets* is played with goat knuckles.

You can make *osselets* from lamb, veal, or beef knuckles. Have an adult boil the bones until the meat falls off. When they're cool and dry, you'll have *osselets*. Or, if you don't have any *osselets*, you can play the game with stones or jacks.

Osselets

Number of players: At least 2

What you'll need: a small ball that will bounce, such as a golf ball

5 *osselets*, jacks, or stones

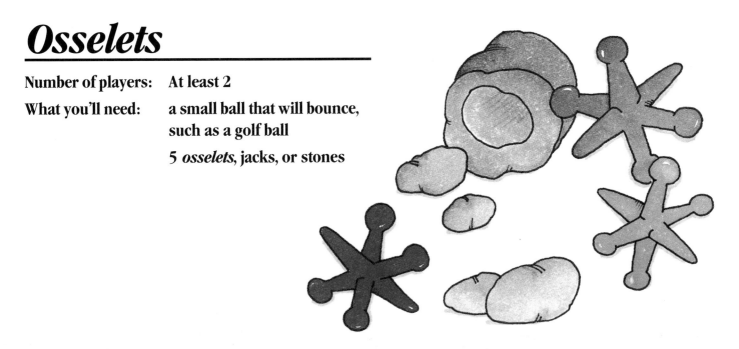

How to play:

1. Pick up the ball and the *osselets*.

2. Toss the ball and the *osselets* into the air so they land on the ground. The ball must be caught after the first bounce.

3. Bounce the ball and pick up an *osselet*. The ball can only bounce once. If you drop the *osselet* or the ball, or if the ball bounces more than once, the turn passes to the next player.

4. Bounce the ball again. Now, keeping the first *osselet* in your hand, pick up a second *osselet* and catch the ball after the first bounce.

5. Keep playing until you've picked up all five *osselets*. The first player to pick up all 5 *osselets* without any misses wins.

Some Hatitian children play *osselets* with *osselets* only and no ball. Here's how:

Toss all five *osselets* on the ground. Pick one up and toss it into the air. While the first one is in the air, pick up a second and catch the first one on the way down. Keep going until all of the *osselets* are picked up.

India

India is the home of the world's second-largest population. Almost 800 million people live there. And India is the movie capital of the world. More than 700 films are made in India each year.

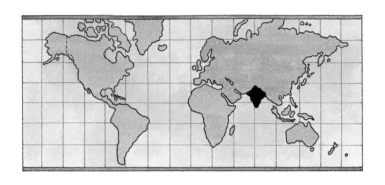

When children play outdoors in India, they often play a game called *kabaddi* (pronounced *kuh-BAH-dee*). It's similar to tag, but all the running and tagging need to be done in one breath. *Kabaddi* can be played in a yard, playground, or *kabaddi* court —or it can be played on a sidewalk.

Kabaddi

Number of players: **6 to 20**

What you'll need: **Rope or chalk to draw a dividing line between each team's territory**

How to play:

1. Players are divided into two equal teams. Flip a coin to see which will be team one and which team two.

2. Teams line up so that each team is about 20 feet (6 meters) from the center dividing line.

3. A player from team one stands near the center line. When the game begins, the player runs into team two's territory and tries to tag a team two player. While doing this, the player must keep yelling "Kabaddi, Kabaddi, Kabaddi..." without taking a breath.

4. Now the player attempts to run back into his or her own territory while continuing to yell "Kabaddi, Kabaddi" without taking a breath.

5. If the player makes it back into his or her own territory, without taking a breath, the player stays in the game. If the player stops shouting "Kabaddi" and takes a breath, then that player can be tagged by an opposing team member. If this happens before the player crosses back into his or her territory, the tagged player is out of the game.

6. It is then team two's turn.

7. The game ends when one team has no players left.

Indonesia

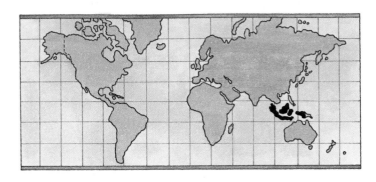

Indonesia includes some 17,000 islands south of the Asian mainland. Some of the islands are located north of the equator. Most are located south of it.

Indonesia's weather is wet and warm all year. During the rainy season, it rains very hard every day. When the rain stops, Indonesian children are eager to play outdoors. One of the games they play is *main karet gelang* (pronounced *main ka-RET ge-LANG*). *Main karet gelang* means "rubber band game." Children make a wad of rubber bands to kick. Then they kick it into the air. In some Asian countries, children play the same game with a badminton birdie, or a homemade item similar to a birdie.

Main Karet Gelang

Number of players: 2 to 10; you can play as individuals, or you can divide the players into teams.

What you'll need: Indonesian children make their clump of rubber bands from about 40 bands tied together in the middle with another rubber band. If you don't have enough rubber bands to make a wad big enough to kick, use a badminton birdie or small ball.

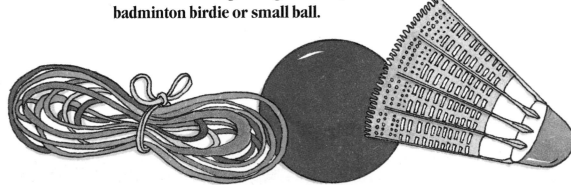

How to play:

1. Toss your rubber band wad, birdie, or ball into the air.

2. Kick it with one foot.

3. Keep kicking the object to keep it in the air so it doesn't hit the ground.

4. Remember to count your kicks, or have an opponent count for you.

5. The player who keeps the object up for the most kicks wins.

Iran

Iran is located in Southwest Asia. It's bounded by Turkey, Iraq, Afghanistan, Pakistan, Armenia, Azerbaijan, and Turkmenistan. Long ago, the country was called Persia.

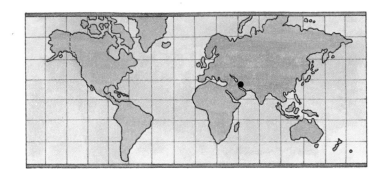

In Iran almost every town has a street bazaar where people buy food, clothing, jewelry, carpets, and almost anything else. You'll also find children playing a form of tag called *haft sang* (pronounced *hahft sang)*, which means "seven stones."

Haft Sang

Number of players: 4 to 12, divided equally into teams

What you'll need: 7 stones, about 3 inches (7.5 centimeters) across

a ball, about the size of a tennis ball

How to play:

1. The players from one team put the stones in a pile.

2. Players from both teams stand scattered from 4 to 6 feet (1 to 2 meters) away from the pile of stones.

3. The players from team two each take a turn trying to knock over the pile of stones with the ball.

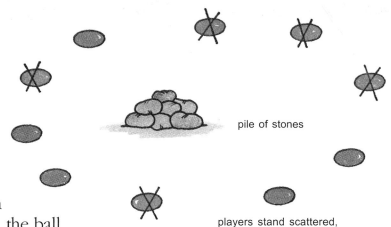

pile of stones

players stand scattered, like in basketbal

4. If a team two player scatters the stones, a team one player must attempt to pile them up again. A team two player tries to stop this by throwing the ball at any team one player–the one who is piling the stones or any other player in the game, particularly those blocking the piler. If the player piling the stones is hit, another takes his or her place. Once a player is hit with a ball, he or she is out.

5. If a player from team one succeeds in piling the stones before all of his or her teammates are tagged out, the team gains a point.

6. The first round ends when team one has succeeded in piling up the stones–or all the players are tagged out by the ball.

7. Then team two piles the stones, and team one tries to knock them over. Once the stones are scattered, a player from team two tries to repile them while team one tries to tag out the team two players by hitting them with the ball.

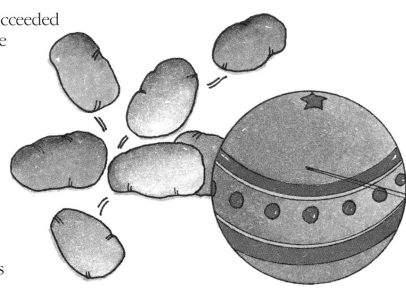

8. There is no specific end to the game. The players usually decide the number of points that will mean a team has won.

Israel

Israel is a land of contrasts. In Tel Aviv, Israel's second-largest city, modern sky-scrapers stand alongside structures built during Biblical times.

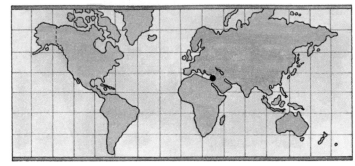

Israel's soil and warm climate are perfect for growing fruits like oranges, lemons, and apricots. Some Israeli children save their apricot pits, which they call *adjuim* (pronounced *ad-joo-EEM*), to use for game pieces.

Here's how to play two games using apricot pits. If you don't have apricot pits and don't want to wait to collect them, you can play these games with marbles.

Adjuim

The Square Game

Number of players: **3 or more**

Equipment needed: **A bag containing an equal number of apricot pits for each player**

How to play:

1. One player is the leader. The leader places four pits in a square, so that the pits are about 1 foot (30 centimeters) apart.

2. Players stand a few feet from the square and try to roll one of their pits into the square.

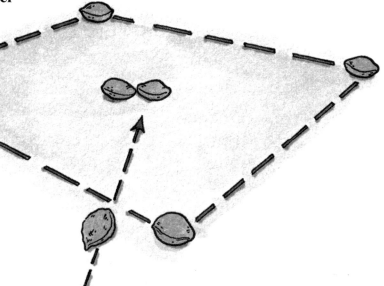

3. When a player's pit lands inside the square, that player keeps all the pits and becomes the new leader.

4. If the player misses, the leader keeps the pit that the player tried to roll into the square.

5. Now another player tries to roll a pit into the square.

6. The game can end at a designated time, and the winner will be the one who has earned the most pits. Or the game can end when one of the players is totally out of apricot pits.

The Jar Game

What you'll need: **a wide-mouthed jar, quart sized or larger**

a bag of apricot pits for each player

How to play:

1. Each player contributes one or two pits to the jar to start the game. The game should begin with at least a dozen pits.

2. Players take turns tossing pits into the jar from a designated distance—3 to 6 feet (90 to 180 centimeters) works best, depending on the age and experience of the players.

3. When a player's pit lands in the jar, he or she wins three pits plus the pit that was tossed.

The game ends when the jar is empty. The winner is the one with the most pits.

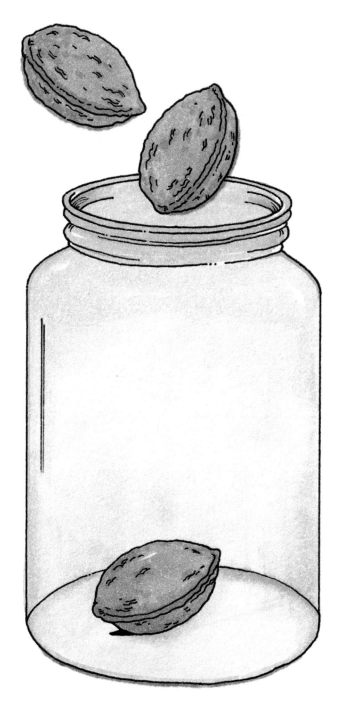

Malaysia

In Malaysia, boys may sit on one side of the classroom and girls may sit on the other. Most Malaysians are followers of Islam, a religion that restricts the contact between boys and girls. So in many parts of Malaysia, girls play with girls and boys play with boys.

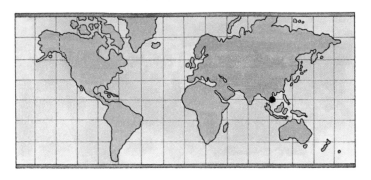

One popular game Malaysian boys play is called *gasing* (pronounced *GAH-sing*). They spin tops as huge as dinner plates inside a circle. *Gasing* is very popular in Malaysia. Some people enter competitions with strict rules.

Gasing

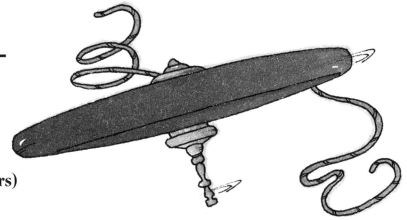

Number of players: At least 2

What you'll need: chalk

a large spinning top

a piece of heavy string, about a yard (90 centimeters) long.

If you don't have a large top, you can make one.

You'll need: 10 paper plates, 12 inches (30 centimeters) in diameter

a pencil (this will be the axle of your top)

2 empty thread spools

a yard of heavy string or ribbon

What to do:

Measure the plates to find the center. You may need adult help for this.

Poke a hole in the center of each plate with the pencil.

Push the plates onto the pencil.

Place one spool over the plates and one under them. If the spools fit too loosely on the pencil, wrap them with rubber bands.

How to play:

1. On the pavement, draw a circle about 10 feet (3 meters) in diameter, wide enough for two tops to spin at once.

2. Tie your piece of string or ribbon to the axle of the top. Now, wind the string tightly around it.

3. Players place their tops inside the circle. They pull their strings to make them spin. The top that knocks the other down is the winner. Or you can play to see whose top spins the longest.

Mali

Mali is located in West Africa. Its name means "the hippopotamus." One of the world's greatest waterways, the Niger River, flows through Mali. Each year, tourists visit Mali to take river journeys on this well-known river.

Mali's population is made up of people from many tribes, whose roots go back thousands of years. So does a common game that tribal children play called *sey* (pronounced *say*). It's a guessing game that involves hiding a pebble.

Sey

Number of players: 2

What you'll need: an area of sand or dirt

one small pebble, which children call the *tibi*

How to play:

1. Draw two concentric circles in the dirt or sand. One circle should be about 20 inches (51 centimeters) in diameter. The other circle should be about 18 inches (46 centimeters). This makes the playing track.

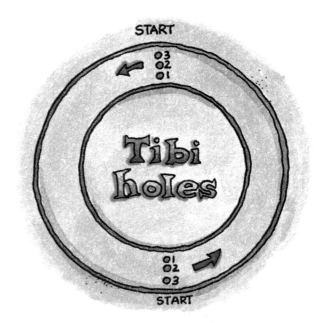

START
03
02
01

Tibi holes

01
02
03
START

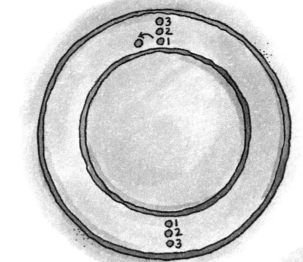

 2. Each player sits on one side of the track. Each player makes three holes about 1 inch (2.5 centimeters) apart between the circles. These are the places where the players can try to hide the *tibi*.

3. Player one takes the *tibi* and some dirt in his or her hand, then hides the *tibi* in one of the three holes that have been made between the circles.

 4. Player two tries to guess where the *tibi* is hidden.

5. If player two guesses correctly, it's his or her turn to hide the *tibi* and make player one guess. If player two guesses incorrectly, then player one gets a point and also gets to hide the *tibi* again.

6. When a player gains a point, the player makes a hole to his or her right, about an inch from the third hole in his or her side of the track. As players gain points, they will make more and more holes that will get closer and closer to the opponent's side of the track.

 7. The game ends when one player has made so many holes that his line connects up with the line of holes that the opponent began with.

Mexico

Mexico's northern border is 2,000 miles (3,200 kilometers) long and shared with the United States. On the south, it's bordered by two Central American countries, Guatemala and Belize. Mexico's official language is Spanish, although some Indians speak their own language. More than fifty languages are spoken in Mexico.

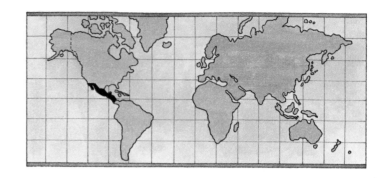

Mexico's most popular sport is *fútbol*. The pronunciation sounds like the American game football, but to Mexicans, *fútbol* means soccer.

Mexican children enjoy many games, which they often play indoors. One is *los hoyos* (pronounced *los O-yos*) which means "the holes."

Los Hoyos

Number of players: 4 to 10

What you'll need: a tennis ball

An area where you can dig a hole for each player. The ball will be rolled into these holes. If an area is unavailable, the balls can be rolled onto a paper plate or into a circle drawn with chalk.

Setup for 5 players

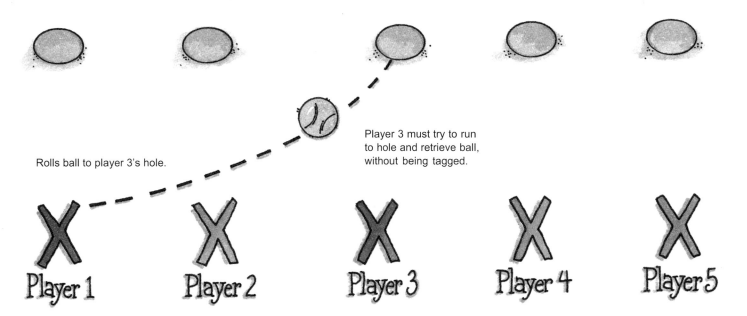

Rolls ball to player 3's hole.

Player 3 must try to run to hole and retrieve ball, without being tagged.

Player 1   Player 2   Player 3   Player 4   Player 5

How to play:

Before the game begins, dig holes, place plates, or draw chalk circles for each player approximately 8 inches (20 centimeters) from each other in a row.

1. Players line up about 10 feet (3 meters) away from the line of holes. The hole in front of each player is that player's hole.

2. The first player rolls the ball into another player's hole.

3. If the player misses, the next player gets a turn.

4. Once a ball lands in a hole, the player whom the hole belongs to must run to retrieve the ball.

5. The other players try to tag the hole owner before the ball is retrieved.

6. If the hole owner retrieves the ball before being tagged, he or she gains a point. If the player is tagged, the turn is over.

7. The ball now goes to player two, until everyone gets a turn.

The Netherlands

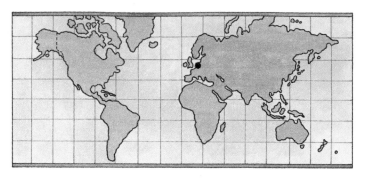

The Netherlands is located in western Europe. The land is very flat and surrounded by water. More than one third of the Netherlands is below sea level. The Dutch word for the Netherlands is *Nederland,* which means lowlands.

The flat land makes the Netherlands a perfect place to bicycle, so just about everyone, young and old, owns a bike. There are so many bicycles that they sometimes cause traffic jams.

The Netherlands' flat terrain is also perfect for playing hopscotch. Dutch children play this game in many versions. One way is days-of-the-week hopscotch. Instead of numbering the squares, children write the names of the days of the week inside the squares.

Days-of-the-Week Hopscotch

Number of players: at least 2

What you'll need: chalk

a marker (a stone or paper clip)

How to play:

1. Draw your hopscotch according to the diagram.

2. Stand in the blank square and toss the marker onto Monday. The marker must land inside the Monday square and not on any other squares or lines or outside the hopscotch. If that happens, the player is out.

3. Stand in the blank square on one foot. Hop over Monday and onto Tuesday, Wednesday, Thursday, and so on. As you hop, you must shout the day you are hopping on. If you forget, or if you shout an incorrect day, you're out and it's the next player's turn. On Sunday, you can stop hopping and rest on two feet.

4. After a rest, you can hop back. Skip over Monday and hop from Tuesday onto the blank square.

5. Toss your marker onto Tuesday. Hop onto Monday, skip Tuesday, and hop directly to Wednesday and finish the week, resting on Sunday. Go back to the blank square, skipping Tuesday.

To really play days-of-the-week hopscotch the Dutch way, write the days of the week in Dutch.

English	Dutch	How to Say It
Sunday	Zondag	ZONE-dahg
Monday	Maandag	MAHN-dahg
Tuesday	Dinsdag	DINS-dahg
Wednesday	Woensdag	WOE-ens-dahg
Thursday	Donderdag	DON-der-dahg
Friday	Vrijdag	VRAY-dahg
Saturday	Zaterdag	ZAH-ter-dahg

6. Repeat the process, tossing markers and jumping until your marker has hit all the days of the week in order. When you've successfully hopped back to the blank square after Sunday, you're done. Remember, when your marker is on Sunday, you don't get a rest!

7. Players lose turns if they step on lines, stumble, or toss the marker improperly into a box. The player leaves the marker on the day last completed and starts on that day at the next turn. Other players must hop over the opponent's marker—in other words, they can't land in that square.

Norway

Norway is located farther north than any other country in Europe. It is known as the Land of the Midnight Sun. Because part of Norway is so far north, during the winter the days are without sun. In the summer, it's light all night and you can see the sun at midnight.

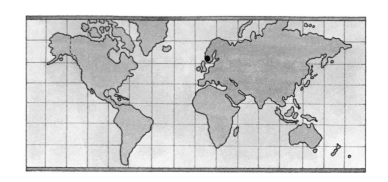

When it's light outside, children play outside their homes. Girls especially enjoy *hoppe-strikk* (pronounced *HOE-peh strik*), which means jump rope made from elastic.

Hoppe-Strikk

Number of players: 3 or more

What you'll need: 4 yards (3.5 meters) of elastic. You can buy this at a fabric store. Sew the ends together to make your jump rope.

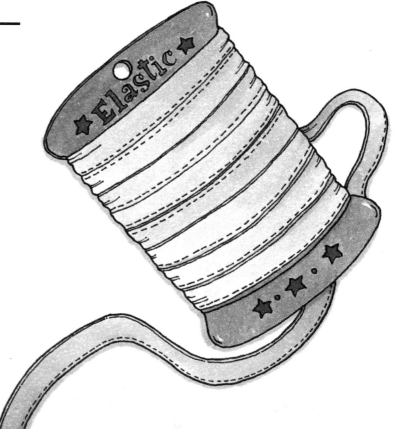

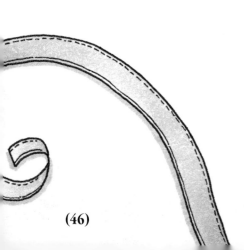

How to play:

1. Two players hold the rope at each end–but not with their hands! They stand with it around their ankles.

2. Players jump over one side and then the other.

3. The holders lift the rope higher and higher.

4. Players jump in and out.

5. Holders can ask players to jump backward, with their eyes shut, or on one foot. When a player misses, he or she is out.

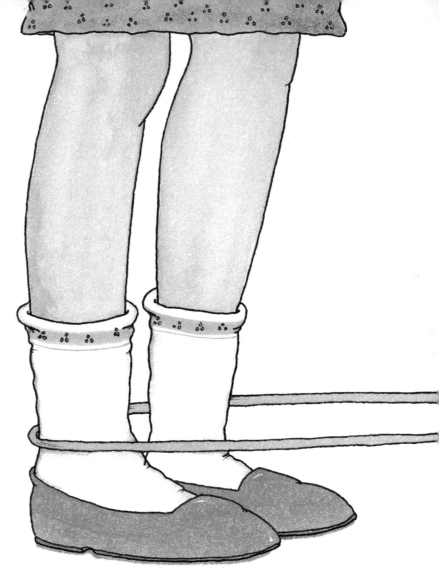

Pakistan

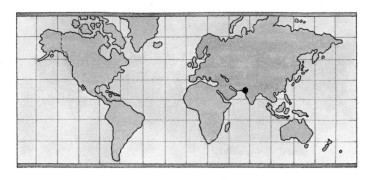

If you lived in Pakistan, you wouldn't need to visit your grandparents because they'd probably live in your house. On Fridays and Saturdays, you'd see your other relatives. Friday is the first day of the weekend and the Sabbath. Saturday is the last day of the week.

On weekends, Pakistani children love to play outside. One popular game is *kokla chhupathi* (pronounced *KOKE-lah chew-PAH-tee*), which is very similar to duck, duck, goose.

Kokla Chhupathi

Number of players: **5 or more**

What you'll need: **a piece of twisted material or handkerchief**

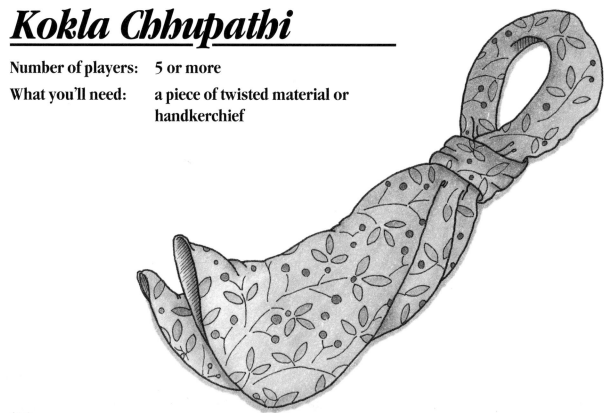

How to play:

1. Players squat in a circle.

2. One player is chosen to be It.

3. It drops the cloth or handkerchief behind a player in the circle.

4. The player who has had the cloth dropped behind him or her, grabs it without turning around. Then the player gets up and chases the player who was It.

5. It runs around the circle, trying to get back to his or her space before being tagged.

6. If It is tagged, he or she remains It. If It reaches his or her place in the circle without being tagged, the player doing the chasing becomes It.

Republic of South Africa

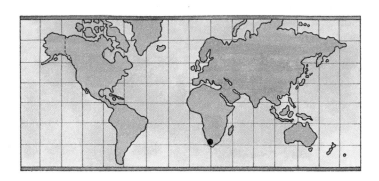

The Republic of South Africa is located on the southern tip of the world's second-largest continent, Africa. The country produces much of the world's gold and diamonds.

South Africa has two official languages, English and Afrikaans. One popular game that South African children play is *drie blikkies* (pronounced *duh-REE BLICK-ees*), which means "three tins" in Afrikaans.

Drie Blikkies

Number of players: 8, in two teams of 4 each

What you'll need: 3 empty tin cans

a tennis ball

chalk

Preparation:

Mark off four posts, about 20 feet (6 meters) from each other.

Mark a circle in the center of the playing area.

Stack the *blikkies* on top of each other at the *blikkie* post.

How to play:

1. Team A has a player standing behind each post, including the *blikkie* post.

2. Team B players line up in the center circle.

3. The first Team B player in line attempts to topple the *blikkies* with the tennis ball. If the player does not topple the *blikkies*, the next player in line tries, until three players have attempted to topple them. Usually the *blikkies* topple, but if they do not, the teams change positions.

4. Once the *blikkies* topple, the player who knocked them over attempts to run from post one to post three.

5. Meanwhile, the Team A player behind the *blikkie* post tries to catch the ball that has just been thrown. That player tosses the ball to the player by the first post.

6. The player at the first post attempts to have the ball in his or her hand before the running player reaches the post, or tag the running player before he or she reaches the post. If not, the ball is tossed to the players behind the second and third posts in that order. These players attempt to get the running player out.

7. If the running player makes it to the post, that team gains a point.

8. If the running player is tagged out, the teams change positions.

9. The team with the most points wins. There's no special number of innings or ending time.

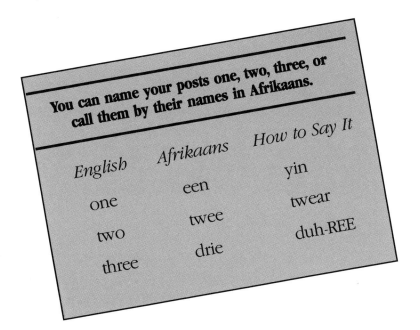

You can name your posts one, two, three, or call them by their names in Afrikaans.

English	Afrikaans	How to Say It
one	een	yin
two	twee	twear
three	drie	duh-REE

Spain

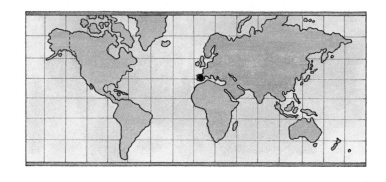

In Spain, the afternoon sun gets so hot that children play inside during most of the day. When the sun begins to go down, Spanish children come outdoors and play in courtyards and on sidewalks.

Spanish children may take advantage of the shadows the sun makes over the trees as it goes down, while playing a tag game called *La Luna y Las Estrellas De La Mañana* (pronounced *lah LOON-a ee lahs es-TRE-yahs day lah man-YA-na*), which means "the moon and morning stars."

La Luna y las Estrellas de la Mañana

Number of players: 3 to 10

How to play:

1. Find a tree that casts a shadow.

2. Choose a person to be *la luna* (moon). That person is It, and has to tag the other players.

3. The rest of the players are *estrellas* (stars).

4. The moon stays inside the shadow made by the tree.

5. The stars run in and out of the tree's shadow. They try to avoid the moon, who tries to tag them.

6. Once the moon captures a star, that star becomes the moon. Then the game begins again.

Sweden

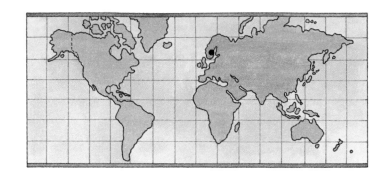

All Swedish children receive free lunch at school. And their doctor and dentist visits are paid for by the government. Swedish adults consider children to be very important people. In Sweden, it's against the law for anyone to hit a child.

Swedish children enjoy playing with marbles. One game involves hitting marbles placed in a pyramid pattern. The Swedish name for this game is *spela kula* (pronounced *spel-LA COO-luh*), which means "playing with balls."

Spela Kula

Number of players: at least 2

What you'll need: a bag of marbles
chalk

How to play:

1. Draw a circle about 10 feet (3 meters) in diameter with chalk.

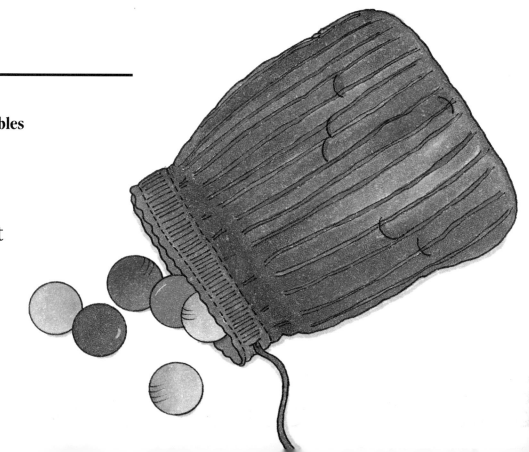

2. The first player piles four marbles into a pyramid formation in the center of the circle.

3. Another player attempts to hit the formation with one of his or her marbles.

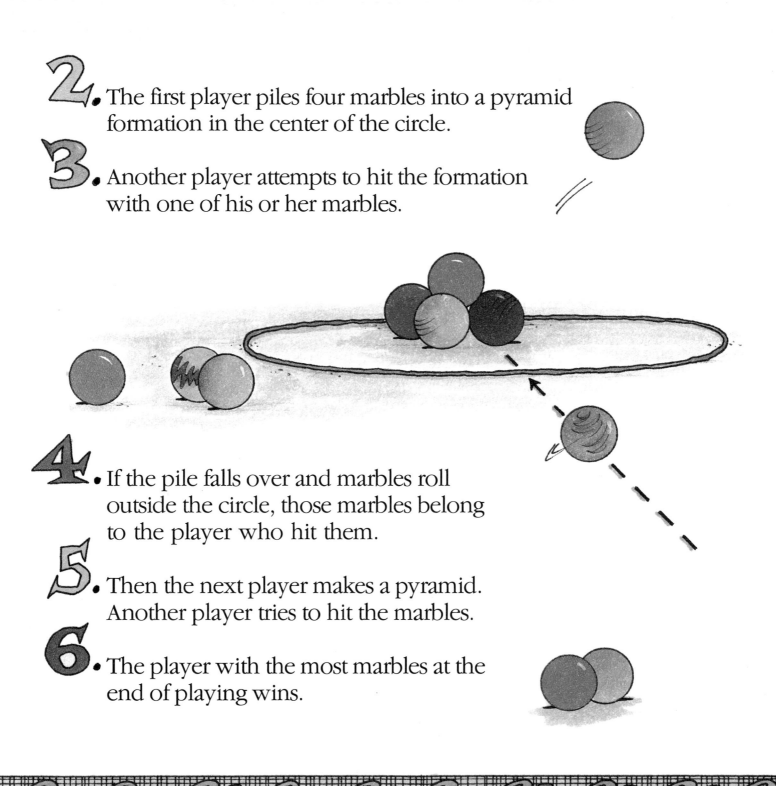

4. If the pile falls over and marbles roll outside the circle, those marbles belong to the player who hit them.

5. Then the next player makes a pyramid. Another player tries to hit the marbles.

6. The player with the most marbles at the end of playing wins.

Thailand

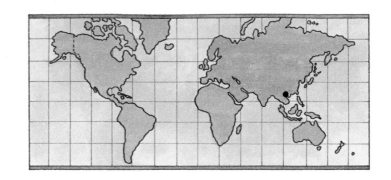

Instead of kissing their parents before they leave for school or play, children in Thailand bow to show great respect for adults. Children in Thailand are considered children longer than in other places in the world. Most Thai people live at home until they're married.

In Thailand, children like to play tag. One version, *Mah Kha Diew* (pronounced *mah kah DEE-o*) is very different from tag games that you already know, because the children tag each other with their feet. The name of the game actually means "horse with one leg!"

Mah Kha Diew

Number of players: 4 or more

What you'll need: chalk

How to play:

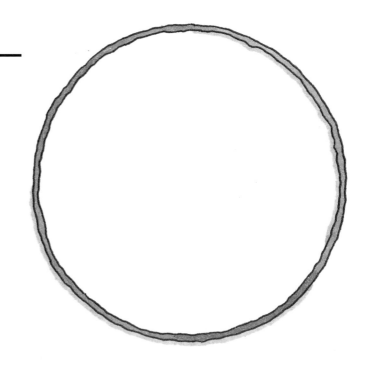

1. Draw a circle with chalk. Make it large enough for all the players to hop in and out of—a diameter of 3 to 6 feet (1 to 3 meters) should work well.

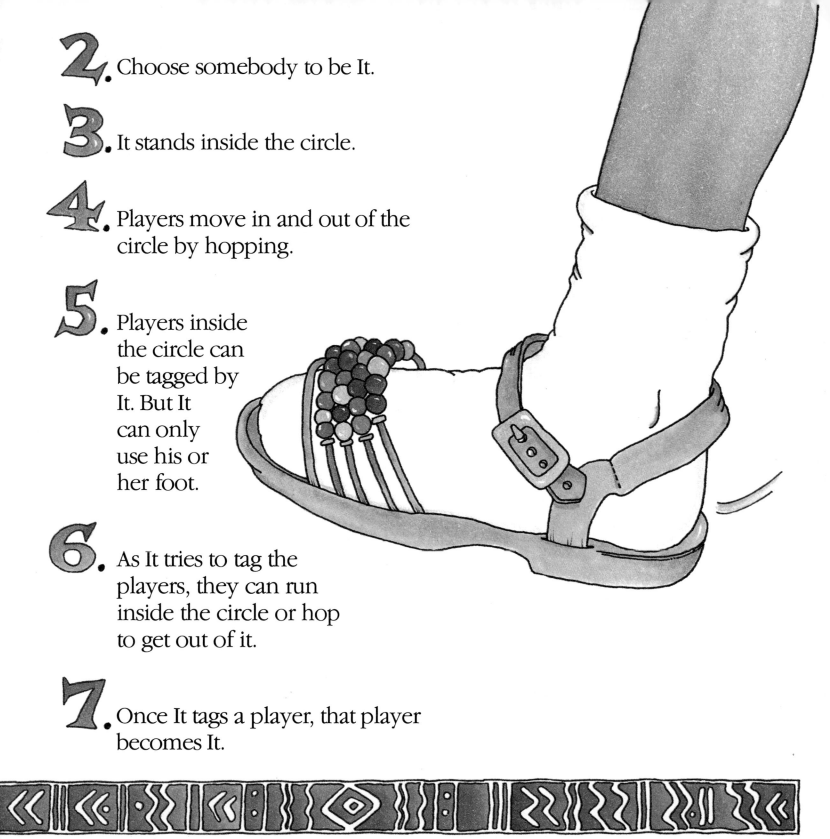

2. Choose somebody to be It.

3. It stands inside the circle.

4. Players move in and out of the circle by hopping.

5. Players inside the circle can be tagged by It. But It can only use his or her foot.

6. As It tries to tag the players, they can run inside the circle or hop to get out of it.

7. Once It tags a player, that player becomes It.

United States

About 80 million children live in the United States. They play hopscotch, tag, hide-and-seek, and jacks. Some games are common in some states or cities but may not be played anywhere else. Other games and rules may differ from town to town.

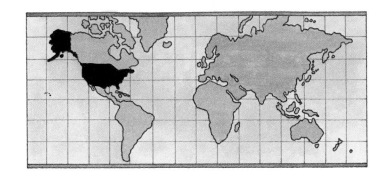

Certain games are very old and may have started in other lands. One very old game that kids still play in cities is kick the can.

Kick the Can

Number of players: **3 to 10**

What you'll need: **chalk**

How to play: **an empty can**

1. Draw a circle large enough so that all the players can stand around it. Put the can in the center of the circle.

2. Choose somebody to be It. The rest of the players stand around the circle.

3. One player goes into the circle and kicks the can as far as possible.

4. Everyone runs and hides except It, who must retrieve the can and run back into the circle.

5. When It reaches the circle, he or she yells "freeze." Everyone stops running exactly where they are. Some players may not have hidden yet, depending on how quickly It retrieves the can and puts it back in the circle.

6. If It sees any player, he or she can call that player's name. Players whose names are called become prisoners. They must stand beside the circle. It must also look for hidden players and attempt to tag them. When It tags a hidden player, he or she becomes a prisoner and must stand beside the circle.

7. The object is for the hidden players to run into the circle and yell "home free" before It can tag them. The best time to do this is while It is away from the circle looking for other players. If It tags them while they are attempting to get into the circle, they become prisoners.

8. Prisoners standing beside the circle may be freed by being tagged by players running into the circle. The freed prisoners must then run into the circle and yell "home free" before It can re-tag them.

9. The last one to enter the circle becomes It, and the game starts again.

Classified Index of Games

By Continent

Europe
Albania
France
Great Britain
The Netherlands
Norway
Spain
Sweden

Africa
Ethiopia
Mali
Senegal
South Africa

The Middle East and Asia
China
Indonesia
India
Iran
Israel
Malaysia
Pakistan
Thailand

Australia
Australia

North America
Canada
Mexico
United States

South America
Argentina
Bolivia
Chile

Central America and Caribbean
Haiti

By Age

K-4th grade
Albania
Argentina
Chile
China
Great Britain
Haiti
India
Israel
Mexico
The Netherlands
Norway
Pakistan
Spain
Sweden
Thailand
United States

Gr 4-up
Bolivia
Canada
Ethiopia
Haiti
Indonesia
Iran
Israel
Malaysia
Mali
South Africa
Sweden
United States

Indoors/Outdoors

All of the games can be played outdoors – but those listed below can be played indoors too. An asterisk indicates the need for a large space such as a gymnasium or large classroom or family room area.

*Argentina	*Great Britain	*India	Malaysia	Norway
*Canada	Haiti	*Indonesia	*Mexico	Pakistan
Ethiopia		Israel		*South Africa

Number of Players Required

1 player	2 players	4 to 10 players	10 or more players
Albania	Albania	Albania	Argentina
China	Bolivia	Argentina	Australia
Haiti	Canada	Australia	Great Britain
Indonesia	Chile	Canada	India
Malaysia	China	China	Iran
The Netherlands	Ethiopia	El Salvador	Pakistan
	France	Great Britain	South Africa
	Haiti	France	Spain
	Indonesia	Haiti	Thailand
	Israel	Indonesia	United States
	Malaysia	Iran	
	Mali	Israel	
	The Netherlands	Mexico	
	Sweden	The Netherlands	
		Norway	
		Pakistan	
		South Africa	
		Spain	
		Sweden	
		Thailand	
		United States	

Bibliography

Abebe, Daniel. *Ethiopia in Pictures*. Minneapolis: Lerner Publications, 1988.

Arnold, Helen. *Postcards From France*. Austin, TX: Raintree Steck-Vaughn, 1990.

Bailey, Donna, and Sprouk, Anna. *Where We Live: Mexico*. Austin, TX: Steck-Vaughn, 1990.

Bender, Lionel. *France*. Morristown, NJ: Silver Burdett Press, 1988.

Bjner, Tamiko. *Children of the World: Sweden*. Milwaukee: Gareth Stevens Publishing, 1987.

Botermans, J., Burrett, T., van Delft, P., and van Splunteren, C. *The World of Games*. New York: Oxford University Press, 1987.

Fox, Mary Virginia. *Enchantment of the World: Iran*. Chicago: Childrens Press, 1991.

Fradin, Dennis B. *Enchantment of the World: Ethiopia*. Chicago: Childrens Press, 1989.

Galvin, Irene Slum. *Chile, Land of Poets and Patriots*. Minneapolis: Dillon Press, 1990.

Gamgee, John. *Journey Through France*. Mahwah, NJ: Troll Associates, 1994.

Ganeri, Anita and Jonardon. *India*. Austin, TX: Raintree Steck-Vaughn Publishers, 1995.

Ganeri, Anita, and Wright, Rachel. *France*. New York: Franklin Watts, 1993.

Gish, Steven. *Cultures of the World: Ethiopia*. Tarrytown, NY: Marshall Cavendish, 1996.

Gofen, Ethel Caro. *France*. North Bellmore, NY: Marshall Cavendish, 1992.

Grunfeld, Frederic V. *Games of the World*. New York: Holt, Rinehart and Winston, 1975.

Hal, Godfrey. *Traditions Around the World: Games*. New York: Thomas Learning, 1995.

Harbin, E. O. *Games of Many Nations*. Nashville: Abingdon Press, 1954.

Hunt, Sarah Ethridge. *Games and Sports the World Around*. Somerset, NJ: Ronald Press, 1964.

Hunt, Sarah Ethridge, and Cain, Ethel. *Games the World Around*. New York: A. S. Barnes, 1941.

Jacobs, Judy. *Indonesia, a Nation of Islands*. Minneapolis: Dillon Press, 1990.

Jacobson, Karen. *A New True Book: Mexico*. Chicago: Childrens Press, 1982.

Jacobson, Karen. *A New True Book: The Netherlands*. Chicago: Childrens Press, 1992.

Kagda, Sakina. *Cultures of the World: Norway*. North Bellmore, NY: Marshall Cavendish, 1995.

Kalman, Bobbie. *China: The People*. Toronto: Crabtree Publishing, 1976.

Kalman, Bobbie. *China: The Culture*. Toronto: Crabtree Publishing, 1989.

Karan, P. O. *India*. Grand Rapids, MI: Gateway Press, Inc., 1988.

Knowlton, Mary Lee, and Sachner, Mark J. *Children of the World: Malaysia*. Milwaukee: Gareth Stevens Publishing, 1987.

Knowlton, Mary Lee, and Wright, David K. *Children of the World: India*. Milwaukee: Gareth Stevens Publishing, 1988.

Kristensen, Preben, and Cameron, Fiona. *We Live in the Netherlands*. New York: The Bookwright Press, 1985.

Lankford, Mary O. *Hopscotch Around the World*. New York: Morrow Junior Books, 1992.

Mauro, Elizabeth L. *Albania*. New York: Chelsea House, 1987.

McNair, Sylvia. *Enchantment of the World: Indonesia*. Chicago: Childrens Press, 1993.

Milberg, Alan. *Street Games*. New York: McGraw-Hill, 1976.

Millen, Nina. *Children's Games From Many Lands*. New York: Friendship Press, 1943.

Milord, Susan. *Hands Around the World*. Charlotte, VT: Williamson Publishing, 1992.

Mulac, Margaret E. *Games and Stunts for Schools, Camps and Playgrounds*. New York: Harper & Row, 1964.

Norbrook, Dominique. *Passport to: France*. New York: Franklin Watts, 1985.

Opie, Iona. *The People in the Playground.* New York: Oxford University Press, 1993.

Opie, Iona and Peter. *Children's Games in Street and Playground.* New York: Oxford University Press, 1969.

Pageman, Robert. *Cultures of the World: Bolivia.* Tarrytown, NY: Marshall Cavendish, 1995.

Pierre, Phillipe. *France.* Milwaukee: Gareth Stevens Publishing, 1989.

Rajendra, Vijeya, and Kaplan, Gisela. *Cultures of the World: Iran.* North Bellmore, NY: Marshall Cavendish, 1992.

Rockwell, Ann. *Games (And How to Play Them).* New York: Thomas Y. Crowell Company, 1973.

Sarin, Amita Vohra. *India: An Ancient Land, a New Nation.* Minneapolis: Dillon Press, 1985.

Schwadach, Karen. *Thailand, Land of Smiles.* Minneapolis: Dillon Press, 1991.

Seward, Pat. *Cultures of the World: Netherlands.* North Bellmore, NY: Marshall Cavendish, 1995.

Sheehan, Sean. *Cultures of the World: Pakistan.* North Bellmore, NY: Marshall Cavendish, 1994.

St. John, Jetty. *A Family in Bolivia.* Minneapolis: Lerner Publications, 1986.

St. John, Jetty. *A Family in Norway.* Minneapolis: Lerner Publications, 1988.

UNICEF. *Hi Neighbor, Book 2: Friendship Road Round the World.* 1960.

Vecchione, Glen. *The World's Best Street & Yard Games.* New York: Sterling Publishing, 1989.

Vecchione, Glen. *The World's Best Outdoor Games.* New York: Sterling Publishing, 1992.

Wiswell, Phil. *Kids Games.* New York: Doubleday, 1987.

Wright, David K. *Enchantment of the World: Malaysia.* Chicago: Childrens Press, 1988.